James Payn

Guide to the Irish Industrial Village and Blarney Castle

James Payn

Guide to the Irish Industrial Village and Blarney Castle

ISBN/EAN: 9783744758567

Printed in Europe, USA, Canada, Australia, Japan

Cover: Foto ©ninafisch / pixelio.de

More available books at **www.hansebooks.com**

GUIDE TO

THE IRISH INDUSTRIAL VILLAGE

AND

BLARNEY CASTLE.

Come and Kiss the Blarney Stone.

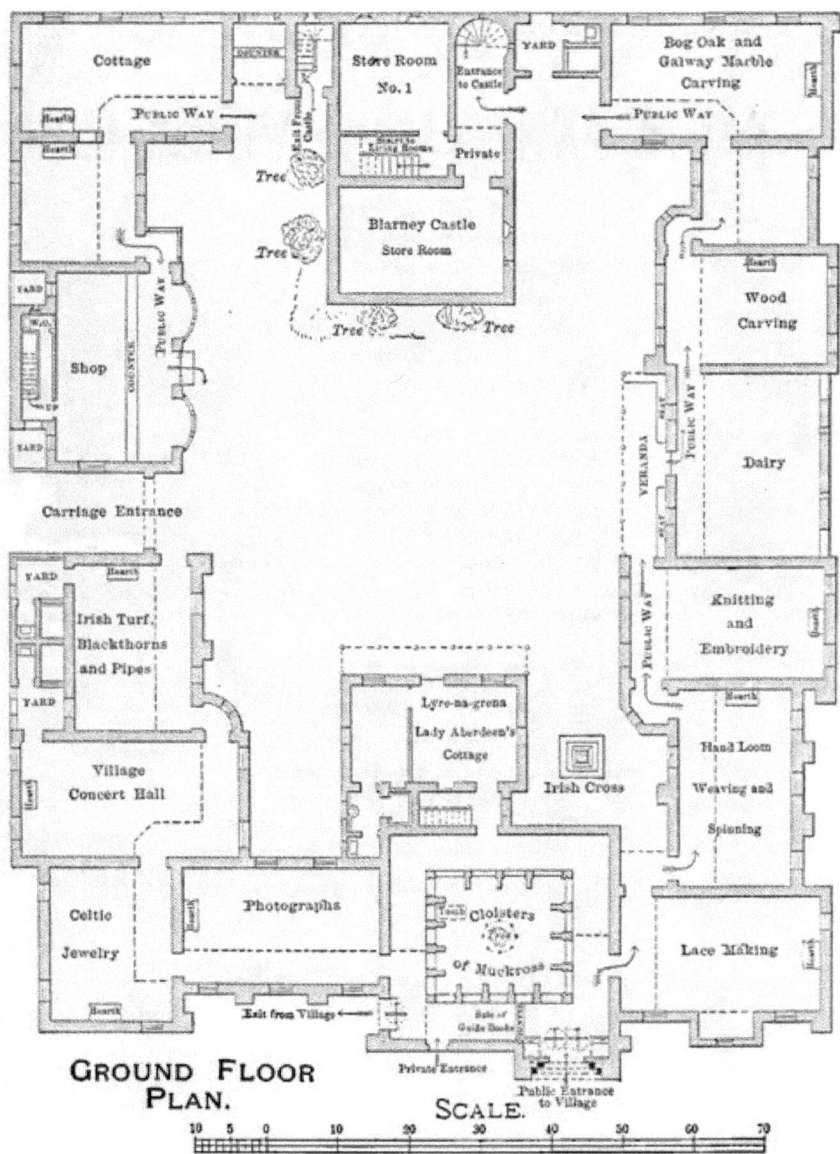

Cottage

COUNTER

Store Room
No. 1

YARD

Bog Oak and
Galway Marble
Carving

← PUBLIC WAY →

Hearth

Hearth

Exit from Castle

Entrance
to Castle

← PUBLIC WAY →

Stairs to
Upper Rooms

Private

Tree

Wood
Carving

Hearth

Blarney Castle
Store Room

Tree

YARD

W.C.

Shop

PUBLIC WAY

Dairy

VERANDA

PUBLIC WAY

YARD

Tree

Tree

Tree

Carriage Entrance

Knitting
and
Embroidery

Hearth

PUBLIC WAY

YARD

Hearth

Irish Turf,
Blackthorns
and Pipes

Lyre-na-grena

Lady Aberdeen's
Cottage

Hearth

Hand Loom

YARD

Irish Cross

Weaving and

Spinning

Village
Concert Hall

Hearth

Celtic

Photographs

Tomb
Tree

Cloisters

of Muckross

Lace Making

Jewelry

Hearth

Hearth

Exit from Village ←

Sale of
Guide Books

GROUND FLOOR
PLAN.

Private Entrance

Public Entrance
to Village

SCALE.

10   5   0   10   20   30   40   50   60   70

OFFICIALS

OF THE

Irish Industrial Village.

PRESIDENT:
THE COUNTESS OF ABERDEEN.

ADVISORY COMMITTEE:
THE EARL OF ABERDEEN.
MR. T. BAKER.
MR. J. J. EGAN.
MR. W. J. HYNES.
MR. A. SHUMAN, BOSTON.
MR. P. J. SEXTON, CHICAGO.
MR. MELVILLE E. STONE, CHICAGO.
MR. JAMES SULLIVAN, CHICAGO.
MR. J. R. WALSH, CHICAGO NATIONAL BANK.

Along with any members of the Dublin Executive or Chicago Committee of the Irish Industries Association who may be in Chicago from time to time.

MANAGER:
MRS. PETER WHITE.

MUSICAL DIRECTOR AND HARPIST:
MISS JOSEPHINE SULLIVAN,
Professor of the Harp at the Academy, Dublin.

ASSISTANT MANAGER:
MR. JOHN ALLEN.

SECRETARY OF THE ASSOCIATION:
MR. CHARLES HATFIELD.

ARCHITECTS:
MR. J. J. EGAN, CHICAGO.   MR. LAURENCE McDONNELL, DUBLIN.

All communications regarding the Village to be addressed to Mrs. White, in care of Lady Aberdeen, Irish Industrial Village, World's Fair, Chicago.

GUIDE TO THE

Irish Industrial Village

AND BLARNEY CASTLE,

THE EXHIBIT OF

The Irish Industries Association

AT THE

WORLD'S COLUMBIAN EXPOSITION, CHICAGO.

President, THE COUNTESS OF ABERDEEN.

"Éire go Brágh."

PUBLISHED BY THE
IRISH VILLAGE BOOK STORE.
1893.

Guide to the Irish Industrial Village.

The entrance to the Irish Village has been copied from the north doorway to the chapel built by Cormac, the bishop king of Munster, in the early part of the twelfth century, which forms part of the wonderful group of ecclesiastical buildings, the ruins of which stand on the Rock of Cashel (the word is derived from *caiseal*—a stone fort), the County Tipperary, and of which a fine complete model will be found within the village. These ruins are beautifully described by the late Mr. Jewitt, in an essay on the remains at Cashel, as follows:

From the midst of a fertile plain in the southern part of the county of Tipperary rises abruptly the immense mass of limestone known as the Rock of Cashel, and which, crowned as it is by lofty and venerable ruins, forms a conspicuous landmark to the surrounding country for many miles.

On nearer approach it increases in grandeur and interest. The town lies at its foot, and the small whitewashed hovels which are nestled under it serve to give interest and contrast to the scene. The rock is inaccessible on all sides except the south, where it is defended by a gateway. On entering within this gateway, and while standing on the green sward at the west end of the building, it is impossible to describe the feelings which crowd upon the imagination; the gray, hoar, and solemn and melancholy-looking ruins seem in their mute eloquence like spirits of the past standing in the present, silent and yet speaking. The ruined cathedral, the shattered castle, and the weather-beaten cross, all raised thoughts which it is not possible to express, and when all these are seen by the light of the setting sun, shining from behind clouds over the distant Galtese, the effect is beyond anything that can be conceived.

The doorway chosen by the architect, Mr. McDonnell, for the entrance of the Irish Village is a singularly fine one. It is round-arched, of five orders, springing from detached shafts, and is surmounted by a high, projecting canopy, divided into panels by perpendicular bands, enriched with zigzag mouldings, and rosettes, and carved heads. Passing through this doorway, with all its associations of the old days of the MacCarthys, the O'Conors, and the O'Brians, we enter the cool cloisters of the far-famed Muckross Abbey, with its tree standing in the midst, bringing to our minds not only the thought of the beautiful, picturesque ruins from which this reproduction is copied, surrounded by its graves of the heroes of bygone days, but also of the exquisite scenery of the surrounding district of Killarney, its mountains, its lakes, its islands.

But the Irish Village at the World's Fair is nothing if it is not practical, and the visitor can not be allowed to muse in the cloisters of Muckross; and so, having provided himself with a guide, he is ushered into the first of the cottages where the inhabitants of this busy little community ply their industries.

And here by the turf-fire over which the potato-pot is hanging can be watched the making of many of the different kinds of lace and crochet-work which is manufactured in Ireland. Ellen Aher trained at the Presentation Convent at Youghal County, makes the beautiful needle-point lace which is so highly prized by those who are its happy possessors; Kate Kennedy illustrates the making of *appliqué* lace as it is done in the cottage homes of Carrickmacross, and Mary Flynn does the same for the much admired fine crochet work made by the poor women around Clones, in County Monaghan, and which is already much appreciated in America; Ellen Murphy shows how the pretty light Limerick lace is made, which is regaining its popularity since Mrs. Vere O'Brien and other ladies and gentlemen have set to work to improve the designs; Bridget McGinley works at her old-fashioned wheel in the next cottage, preparing the wool for Patrick Fagan from Donegal to weave into those delightful homespuns whose merits have been found out of late years by the fashionable world, as well as by the sportsman and athlete; Maggie Dennehy, who talks real Irish, also sits near by and shows how Miss Fitzgerald has taught the women of Valencia Island, County Kerry, to earn their livelihood by knitting.

The "*Teach-boinne*," or dairy, next engages our attention, and here we find Johanna Doherty, Kate Barry, and Maria

Connolly showing us all the delights of a well-trained dairy-maid's profession, and what dainty and appetizing results can be turned out by a deft pair of hands with the aid of the convenient recently-introduced dairy utensils in comparison with the older-fashioned methods, which are also illustrated. A great effort has lately been made in Ireland to improve and develop the butter-making industry, with very promising results. The Hon. Horace Plunkett, M. P., one of the active members of the Irish Industries Association, has taken a hand in this work. The three dairy-maids at the Village have been trained at the Munster Dairy School, an excellent institution near Cork, where all branches of scientific agriculture are taught, to the great benefit of the people.

Mary Fagan makes torchon lace on a pillow, and Mary Cosgrove from Bagnalstown, where Mrs. Edward Ponsonby has founded a centre for the making of embroideries, displays the making of the work to which they have been trained; in another of these cottages, with their quaint, old-fashioned furniture and open roof, will be found a photograph store, from whence many a memory of Ireland and its beauties can be carried away.

The bog-oak-carving industry is one well known to the tourist in Ireland, and is illustrated in the village, both in process of making and in its fully finished state, at the *Darra-bochta* store presided over by Miss Goggin of Dublin, who has also a variety of beautiful specimens of the green Galway marble jewelry.

Michael Nicholas, too, shows the results that are being reaped from the various wood-carving and metal-working classes set on foot in Ireland by the Home Arts and Industries Association, thus providing a paying and profitable occupation for the boys and men as well as the women and girls.

And then comes Blarney Castle. Details concerning the traditions of this well-known place and its stone are given further on in this Guide, and we content ourselves therefore with saying that while the interior of the castle has been set apart as for living and sleeping rooms for the village workers, a winding staircase is provided for the visitors who desire to kiss the magic stone and to get "a view of all Ireland" from the battlements, where a relief map, kindly loaned by Sir

Patrick Keenan and made by Mr. T. W. Conway, B. A., of Dublin, will give to visitors an accurate idea of the surface and extent of the country.

Any bad results from the fatigue of the ascent and descent have been provided against by the "Tigosda," presided over by Mr. Ryan at the foot of the staircase, where he is entirely willing to refresh the hungry and thirsty climbers. They will then feel prepared to visit the "*Sheeppa*," where Miss Mayne, and Miss Robinson, and Miss Keane will show specimens of all manner of cottage industries, and not only lace and embroideries of many kinds, but hosiery and underclothing, woollens and baskets from Letterfrack, and we know not what besides. But the round is not yet complete. There is the Village Music Hall, where Miss Josephine Sullivan, the youthful professor of the harp, from the Dublin Academy of Music, discourses sweet music on the national instrument with a sympathetic touch such as would surely bring joy to the spirit of her patriot father, the late A. M. Sullivan; and in company with her we find many sweet singers of Ireland's national airs, and, needless to say, the Irish piper and the jig dancers. And then, too, there is Tara's Hall, where Mr. Edmond Johnson's (of Dublin) interesting Celtic jewelry is to be seen in the making and in the finished state—models of the Tara brooch and the fibula and other delicate emblems which have been reproduced by this gentleman's zeal on behalf of the antiquities of his country. The model of the ancient Celtic cross erected in a grassy corner of the village square, the loan from Messrs. Colles' marble works at Kilkenny, must also be visited, bringing to mind the fact of the early civilization and art of Ireland, thus showing, even in those far-away days, how full of skill, delicate refinement, and artistic taste were her people.

Lyra-ne-grena, or "The Sunny Nook," is the name which has been given to the cottage standing opposite to the castle, where Lady Aberdeen has her abode when at the village, and in whose rooms may be found specimens of beautiful old Irish furniture, a lovely mantel-piece from an old Dublin house, old Irish prints, books on Ireland presented by Lady Ferguson, Miss Margaret Stokes, and Mrs. O'Connell, and by Messrs. Sealy, Bryers, and Walker, for Lady Aberdeen's village library. In Lady Aberdeen's absence, Mrs. Peter White, the widow of the late Honorable Secretary of the Irish Industries Association, who organized this village, and whose loss is so deeply lamented, acts as her representative and lives in this cottage, which is copied from one at Rushbrook, near Queenstown.

Before leaving finally, a visit must be paid to the village museum, where a very fine set of photographs of Irish antiquities, by Lord Dunraven, arranged and published by Miss Margaret Stokes, the well-known antiquarian, are hung; besides many other objects of interest to Irish hearts which will be lent from time to time during the World's Fair. And surely, surely it is not necessary to suggest that no visitor with Irish sympathies will depart without having set foot on Irish turf, and without carrying away a native blackthorn as a memento of this bit of "Ould Ireland" in the New World!

Ishbel Aberdeen

The Irish Industries Association.

(INCORPORATED.)

The Irish Industries Association, which has undertaken this reproduction of an Irish Village at the World's Fair, was formed by the Countess of Aberdeen in 1886, during the period that the Earl of Aberdeen was Viceroy, with the following objects:

"To organize the Home, Cottage, and other Industries of Ireland, and to bring the various centres of these industries into communication with one another.

"To make arrangements whereby good designs may be brought within the reach of workers in all parts of Ireland.

"To collect and to circulate in Ireland information as to Home or Cottage Industries carried on in other countries, and as to suitable markets for Irish work. To promote the establishment of local centres and committees, and to help and advise generally. To facilitate the exhibition and sale of work, and the provision of the best implements and material at wholesale prices.

"To make arrangements with the carrying companies for the speedy transit of goods at the lowest possible rates.

"To foster the use of all good Irish manufactures, and the production for home use of such articles as can be conveniently made in the homes of the people.

"To forward, as far as possible, the improvement and development of existing Irish industries, and the introduction of other industries which are likely to be useful or profitable.

"To insist on the great need that exists for industrial instruction and training, and, as far as possible, to promote the same in the general education of the people.

" To receive donations, subscriptions, and bequests from persons desiring to promote the objects aforesaid, or any of them, and to hold funds in trust for the same.

" To construct, alter, and maintain any buildings necessary or convenient for the purposes of the association.

" To do all such other lawful things as may from time to time be conducive to the attainment of the objects above set forth, or any of them."

During the seven years that the association has been at work it has been able to make considerable advance toward these aims:

(1.) It has brought the Cottage and Home Industries of Ireland into communication with a common centre.

(2.) It has provided designs, and given courses of art training as far as its means have allowed.

(3.) It has drawn the attention of the public to the industries carried on in Ireland, and to the excellence of their products.

(4.) It has obtained trade orders for the workers.

(5.) It has held sales, and has established two depots, one at 14 Suffolk Street, Dublin, and the other at 20 Motcomb Street, London, for the selling of Irish goods, and has, through these means, sent much money direct into the homes of the peasantry. During last year $25,000 were thus forwarded to the workers.

(6.) It has lately established several local centres for the further development of industries suitable to the different districts.

(7.) It has done much to bring home to the workers the need for business-like habits, uniform excellence of work, and last, but not least—

(8.) It has formed a platform on which persons of the most diverse political and religious views meet together in a common work, which all acknowledge to be for the good of their country.

To show that this is no idle boast, a glance at the names of those who form the council, the Executive of the Association, will be sufficient. There we find as an active member the wife of the Conservative Viceroy, Lord Londonderry, as well as the Home Rule Viceroy, Lord Aberdeen; there we find Cardinal Logue, Archbishop of Armagh, and also the Protestant Archbishop of Dublin; there, too, are John Dillon, beside Hon. Horace Plunkett, the Unionist member for Dublin; there we find the Parnellite Lord Mayor of Dublin and Alderman Meade, beside William O'Brien, and Michael Davitt; and so we might go on, giving instances from both the central and the local committees, and from the list of stall-holders at the sales, showing how Roman Catholics, Episcopalians, Presbyterians, Methodists, Quakers, all join hands in this work, as well as Nationalists and Unionists of all sections.

A good illustration of this feature of the association was shown at an influential meeting held at Dublin in support of the Irish Village, when the present Home Rule viceroy, Lord Houghton, took the chair; when, in the course of a sympathetic and eloquent speech, he laid stress on this point:

"If you look at this platform," he said, "and you have a better opportunity of observing it than I have, you will see that the materials, so to speak, of which it is composed are what in coal-mining we should call distinctly inflammable [laughter]. But in the words 'Irish Industries' we have a safety-lamp which, I am confident, prevents any risk whatever of accidents. [Hear! hear!]

"It is, indeed, seriously speaking, a very great pleasure to me to find how completely people of very divergent views can sink their differences and combine for the furtherance of an admirable object, such as that before you." [Applause].

At another meeting in support of the Irish Industries Association and the Irish Village, held in London, the Unionist landlord, Lord De Vesci, took the chair, and Lady Aberdeen, the Hon. Horace Plunkett, the Unionist, and the eloquent Hon. Edward Blake, the Nationalist, spoke. Some letters of apology which were read at that meeting may also interest our readers, as showing the sympathy of Mr. Gladstone, Mr. Arthur Balfour, and Mr. John Morley with the movement.

10 Downing Street
Whitehall

Mch 3. 1893

My dear Lady Aberdeen

The end of this week
is devoted to Brighton and
I shall not be able to attend
your meeting next Satur-
day on behalf of Irish Industries. But I heartily con-
gratulate on the company you
are to assemble, as well as
on the progress you have made.

and I shall watch with
great interest the future
proceedings in this important
matter Believe me
    Most sincerely yours
        WEGladstone
The
Countess of Aberdeen

4, CARLTON GARDENS, S. W., 3d March, 1893.

DEAR LADY ABERDEEN: I am sorry that my absence from town to-morrow makes it impossible for me to be present at your meeting. I particularly regret that this should be so, as I should have been glad to do anything in my power in furtherance of the important work in which you are engaged.

Believe me yours sincerely,

Arthur James Balfour

MARCH 3, 1893.

DEAR LADY ABERDEEN: I wish very much that I could have been present at the meeting of the Irish Industries Association; but my time is pre-occupied. You know that I have always watched the work done in connection with Irish industries with lively interest, and I most heartily wish you well in so excellent an enterprise.

Yours very truly,

John Morley.

Before starting for America, Lord and Lady Aberdeen received many letters wishing them godspeed in their enterprise at Chicago.

The following are a few specimens:

His Grace Doctor Walsh, Archbishop of Dublin, writes:

I need hardly add that you have my best wishes for the success of your interesting enterprise in connection with the Irish Village at Chicago.

By this time you should hardly stand in need of a letter of introduction to any one in the States, whether American or Irish, who takes an interest in the prosperity of Ireland. But if there is any quarter in America in which you think an introduction from me may in any way be of help to you, or to the work in which you are laboring so devotedly and with such disinterested and untiring zeal, you know you are very welcome to use this letter for the purpose.

With kindest remembrances to Lord Aberdeen, I remain, dear Lady
Aberdeen.   Most faithfully yours,

+ William J. Walsh
Archbishop of Dublin

His Eminence Cardinal Logue, Archbishop of Armagh,
writes:

ARA CŒLI, ARMAGH, April 15, 1893.

MY DEAR LADY ABERDEEN: I have great pleasure in bearing testi-
mony to the grand work which the Association is doing. I feel that its
success hitherto has been mainly due to the untiring zeal with which
your ladyship, aided and encouraged by Lord Aberdeen, have labored
to promote industries among the Irish people. I know that the Irish
people are deeply grateful to you and your noble husband for efforts
both have made to promote their comfort and prosperity. I trust that
the fresh efforts you are making, especially your great undertaking in
connection with the Chicago Exhibition, will meet with the signal success
which they merit.

Wishing your ladyship and Lord Aberdeen a prosperous voyage, a
safe return, and all those blessings which your zeal for the welfare of the
poor can not fail to secure for you,

I am, dear Lady Aberdeen,

Yours faithfully,

+ Michael Card. Logue

Lord Plunket, Protestant and Conservative Archbishop
of Dublin, writes:.

THE PALACE, ST. STEPHEN'S GREEN,
DUBLIN, April 15, 1893.

DEAR LADY ABERDEEN: I write for the purpose of expressing my
very deep interest in the efforts you are so nobly making to have our Irish
industries fairly and prominently represented at the Chicago Exhibition.
Most heartily do I wish for the success of the Irish Village, and most
truly, in common with multitudes of all creeds, classes, and political

opinions in Ireland, do I thank you for your self-sacrificing labors on behalf of my native land!

Yours sincerely,

Plunket Dublin

Mr. Justin McCarthy writes:

APRIL 15, 1893.

DEAR LADY ABERDEEN: Most cordially do I wish you success in your Chicago enterprise. I have the most thorough sympathy with your objects, and I believe in the soundness of your methods. Other methods may do well also—and we have need of everything that can be done—yet I can testify to the entire sincerity of your purposes and to their truly *national* character on behalf of Ireland and Irish industrial interests.

Very truly yours,

Justin McCarthy

Mr. Michael Davitt, M. P., writes:

Needless to say that my heartiest good wishes go with you for the success of all your plans at Chicago. I fully believe you *will* succeed beyond your expectations.

Michael Davitt

These letters and expressions of sympathy might be multiplied, but they, along with the extraordinary manifestations of interest and enthusiasm in the movement, shown at all public meetings in Ireland, at which Lady Aberdeen explained the plans and the objects of the Irish Village, are sufficient to show how all Ireland is watching the enterprise and feels concerned in its success.

Mr. William Redmond, M. P., also cabled his good wishes for the opening of the Irish Village, and Mr. James Carew was only prevented at the last moment from coming out personally to help forward the undertaking.

On the day of Lord and Lady Aberdeen's departure from Queenstown leading articles appeared in the *Freeman's Journal*, the *Independent*, and the *Irish Times*, all conveying Ireland's good wishes, and calling on the Irish in America to coöperate by every means in their power to promote this effort on behalf of the Irish peasantry. The promoters of "Ould Ireland" at the World's Fair are not afraid but what they will receive this support and coöperation heartily and ungrudgingly from those who so unceasingly remember the loved land from which they sprang. They gratefully acknowledge the many tokens of support they have already received, and especially the spontaneous and ungrudging interest of the press.

The practical sympathy shown by His Eminence Cardinal Gibbon, and their Graces Archbishop Feehan, Archbishop Ireland, and Archbishop Ryan has been of the utmost value. These prelates have ordered vestments, which are now exhibited, and which will, we trust, draw many others of the American Catholic clergy to follow their example.

The Archbishop of Chicago has also kindly allowed us to print the following letter:

CHICAGO, May 15, 1893.

THE COUNTESS OF ABERDEEN.

DEAR MADAM: I regret very much that, having had so many engagements, I have not yet been able to visit the Irish Village at the Exposition. The establishment of it is a very noble and most praiseworthy undertaking. I hope your labor will be most amply rewarded, and that you will find in America a cordial sympathy in your efforts in behalf of Irish industries.

I remain, dear madam, with the greatest respect,

✝ P. A. Feehan
Abp. Chicago

Aberdeen

We have also to convey our most cordial and grateful thanks to Mr. J. Walsh of the Chicago National Bank, Mr. P. J. Sexton and Mr. A. Shuman of Boston, who, along with the Hon. Horace Plunkett, M. P., Sir John Arnott of Cork, and Mr. James Talbot Power of Dublin, have each generously advanced $5,000 to the fund, and to Lord Aberdeen, who advanced $7,500. Many other smaller sums have been both given and advanced by kind friends on both sides of the Atlantic. At the close of the Fair a full balance sheet will be published, and it is hoped that by that time not only the guarantors will have safely received back their loans, which have been of such vital service, but that a handsome surplus will be at the credit of the Irish Industries Association for the further carrying on of its work in Ireland.

These few words can not be concluded without drawing attention to the ability shown in the design of the village, as drawn out by the rising young Dublin architect, Mr. Laurence McDonnell; and without acknowledging our great indebtedness to our kind and generous architect in Chicago, Mr. J. Egan, who has carried out the plans with so much personal interest and skill and care, and to Mr. P. J. Sexton for the unceasing and vigilant assistance which he has given to the village, both during its construction and in its finished state.

ISHBEL ABERDEEN.

AN ODE

FOR THE OPENING OF THE IRISH VILLAGE AT CHICAGO.

BY MISS KATHERINE TYNAN.

Columbus, hailing first this land asleep,
Far in the purple deep,
O'er coral islands and o'er winds of dawn
And sapphire veils withdrawn,
Foresaw not where did lie
Wide lakes to mirror half a splendid sky
And sword-like hills to cleave the clouds in sunder,
And falls like thunder
Roaming down many a terrible ravine;
Nor that the cliffs, quiet as drowsing kine,
Hid his highway to a new continent,
O! Land unspent!
Land of the world's youth and the sun's old age!
Magnificent heritage
Which Spain's great Saint-Commander gave the world.
With flags unfurled
For joy, not war, with martial beat of drum,
The Old World's nations come,
All in exceeding peace and amity,
To clasp firm hands with thee.

He, the great Captain, could he see, would smile,
Lifting his limbs the while,
On which the shackles of a Spanish cell
Had left their marks too well,
Only that in those years in heaven each weal
Had time to close and heal
And grow a glory like a scarlet rose,
Would smile, remembering those
His rude rebellious sailors, and their awe
When at the last they saw
Low on the sky their promised paradise
Gleam and arise.
Yea, he would smile, remembering how he lay
In dungeons dark and gray,
With wash of rotting water to his knees,

(28)

For where the bison roamed beneath the trees,
And the gray bear lay in his fetid den,
Lo, men and men and men!
Glory and greatness of the human race,
And freedom, bright of face,
All arts and industries,
And brotherhood and peace!

We, too, the sunset's children, and your kin,
With but the seas between,
Seeing we have built your cities with our hands
And delved your fruitful lands,
And with your wounds have bled,
And sown your battle-fields with Irish dead.
We, too, have part in this your jubilation
And great commemoration,
Marching in rank with the world's army vast,
Endlessly marching past,
Army of peace and love and brave endeavor,
Great as a new world ever.

We, too, like old Columbus did set sail
On a propitious gale,
Out of a night of hunger and of cold,
Seeking, like him of old,
The El Dorado that should change the world,
And sailed and sailed away, while tempests hurled
Their shafts upon us, and as timbers flew.
O New World, it was you,
Star of our hope, that then
Lit the horizon, flawless, without stain,
Like a most pure and perfect amethyst
Set in a golden mist.
Breathless, like him we heard it loud and low,
Land, ho! Land, ho!

Land of our hope!
And light ashine in many a horoscope!
And great beneficent land that welcomes in
The exiles, fierce and thin,
From Old World chains and Old World hunger keen!
Land of the West!
More than thy sons rise up and call thee blest!

From glens where only foot of goat should tread,
Or little mountain sheep that sweetly fed
Among the stones where a chance grass-blade springs;

From hills, where eagles' wings
Winnow the darkness are we come;
And from the creeping foam;
From wastes of peat, where screams for food
The seagull hungry for her brood,
That fears to dive
Into the shrieking sea, where curls alive
The green waves springing for their prey;
From pleasant valleys, pastures gay,
Brighter than emeralds, are we come
To our lost kinsmen's home.

Here they are free,
All the wide world is free from sea to sea;
Here they are part
Of a great nation's mother-jealous heart,
Jealous for her least child's least dignity,
Here they are free!
(Save for heart hunger that perpetually
Calls them across the foam,
Voice of their mother crying, come home, come home!
Out of the sea-fog and the mist
Her wild voice hath not ceased).
Now, not for riches or for greatness, we
Praise thee, Columbia free,
But that thou art enthroned in the West,
With thy large mother-limbs and mother-breast,
Thy kind eyes and the sunlight on thy hair,
Mother of nations fair!
Glory to God who made thee beautiful,
And rich and wise to rule,
And gave thee where thou art
Thy great maternal heart,
Glory! glory!
His blessing still be shed on thee,
And all men's praise be thine eternally,
And his who did discover
Thee, thy true knight and lover!

SELECTION OF THE FITTEST;

Or, How Irish Colleens Were Chosen to Represent Ireland at the World's Fair.

A TOUR ON BEHALF OF THE IRISH VILLAGE.

BY ANGUS MACKAY.

On Friday, February 10, 1893, Lady Aberdeen, accompanied by her titled twelve-year-old daughter, Lady Marjorie Gordon, and the late Mr. Peter White, Honorary Secretary to the Irish Industries Association, commenced a tour through Ireland, round various centres of Irish industries which were to be represented at the Irish Village at Chicago. The tour extended over ten days, during which Lady Aberdeen visited many lace and crochet makers working in their cottages; inspected convent and industrial schools where lace, crochet-making, embroidery, weaving, knitting, etc., is taught; received and replied to addresses presented to her by public boards constituted of men of all creeds and shades of political opinion, and with the assistance and coöperation of Mr. White organized committees and formed local branches of the Irish Industries Association in Clones, Limerick, Cork, and other centres. The tour from first to last was successful and profitable, for it was the means of further organizing and developing the work of the Irish Industries Association in Ireland, and also of bringing prominently before the country the real objects of the Irish Village at the World's Fair, and thereby obtaining a large measure of support for it, both financial and personal.

The first place that claimed Lady Aberdeen's attention was Carrickmacross, where the celebrated lace of that name is manufactured by the peasant women in their humble homes. This industry was first taught to the people of that district fifty-eight years ago by a Miss Reid of Rahans

House, who happened to find a piece of old Flemish lace. She first solved the mystery of its manufacture herself and then imparted her knowledge to a class of young women, who were apt to learn. Thus originated the famous Carrickmacross lace, known now all over the world where fashions have a place in the thoughts of ladies. Several splendid specimens of the beautiful fabric are on exhibition in the

A BRIGHT WORKER.

Irish Village, in the Woman's Building: Lady Aberdeen, accompanied by Mrs. Browne of Dublin, one of the most earnest workers on the Committee of the Irish Industries Association, visited the workers in their homes, with Lady Marjorie, Mr. White, Miss McKeon, who overlooks the work in this district, Dean Biermingham, and some other priests in the district, and saw them plying the needle by the little windows, which do not admit much light to the cottage. Many beautiful lace flounces and veils were examined with interest, and several photographs of the lace-makers at their work were taken by Lady Aberdeen. The cottages where the lace-makers live are scattered over a wide area in the neighborhood of Carrickmacross, and having paid a short visit to each, and having selected a capable worker for the Irish Village, the party drove into the town itself, where the members of the Board of Guardians and the members of the Town Commissioners presented Lady Aberdeen with an address. The visitors went around the Bath and Shirley Schools, where the lace-

JUST CAUGHT BY THE KODAK.

makers are trained, and the Convent Schools, and were entertained at luncheon before returning to Dundalk, where the night was passed and where more Industrial Schools were inspected. That evening in Dundalk Lady Aberdeen and her daughter had the pleasant experience of being serenaded by the town band by torch-light.

Early next morning the Countess and her party departed for Clones. The chairman and members of the Clones Town Commissioners and several clergymen met and welcomed her ladyship, and hundreds of the townsfolk assembled out-

3

side the station and gave their guests a *Cead mille failthe*. In the course of the forenoon Lady Aberdeen and Mr. White conferred with the leading citizens on the subject of the improvement of the crochet industry in the district, and suggestions were made as to the best way of developing the work, such as the supplying of the best thread to the crochet-makers; the bringing of the workers into a market without the intervention of a middleman, who would swallow all the profits; the supply of new designs, and so on. It was pointed out that the Irish Industries Association was one of the best

WHERE A BRIDAL SET OF CARRICKMACROSS LACE WAS MADE.

mediums for selling the crochet and for obtaining further orders for it from the trade, and was also in a position to furnish fresh designs. The conference resulted in the ladies and gentlemen present determining there and then to form a local committee and branch of the association to look after the industry. The committee was constituted of gentlemen and ladies of all sections of the community, the chairman of the Town Commissioners undertaking to act as chairman, and Mr. Robinson, the town clerk, becoming secretary. Afterward a public meeting was held in the town hall, attended by hundreds of workers from the mountainous district around, when several addresses were presented to Lady Aberdeen. Among the gentlemen who spoke were Catholics, and Protestants, and ministers of all denominations. Lady Aberdeen herself made a speech which gave much information about the work and also the Irish Village, and in which reference was made to the extensive orders which Mr. White had obtained in America for Clones' crochet-work. Mr. White frequently made journeys to America on behalf of the Irish Woollen Company, and on the last of these occasions he secured orders for crochet that for many months kept some two hundred women employed at a time when but for this timely help starvation would have stared them in the face. After the meeting Lady Aberdeen, having engaged Mary Flynn to come out to Chicago to show the crochet-making, returned to Dublin and spent the Sunday at the castle. Early on Monday morning, the noble lady, with her daughter and Mr. White, travelled to Limerick, where on leaving the train she received a great popular ovation, and was escorted triumphantly by hundreds of the citizens to the city hall, where the mayor and aldermen and councilors, wearing their robes, received her and presented her with an address. In a voice full of emotion Lady Aberdeen replied, and expressed her thanks. Luncheon was partaken of at the palace of the Protestant Bishop of Limerick, Dr. Graves, and subsequently Lady Aberdeen met at the Chamber of Commerce the leading merchants and business men of the city, gentlemen of all creeds and of all political faiths. From these citizens she received an address which bore the names of Lady Emly, Lord and Lady Monteagle, Mr. Bannatyne, the President of the Chamber of Commerce, Mr. A. A. Shaw, Vice-President, and many others. The Countess having replied to the address, resolutions in support of the Irish Industries Association were adopted. Later in the afternoon, according to the arrangement made by Mr. White, visits were paid to Mr. Shaw's celebrated bacon factory, and to one of the chief hospitals, and later in the evening Lady Aberdeen received at the palace a number of the old and genuine Limerick lace-makers, who are now employed by Mrs. Vere O'Brien, who has done so much for Limerick lace; one of these, who said she was eighty-six years of age, is the sole survivor of the four women who worked the bridal-veil for Queen Victoria. On Tuesday visits were paid to Mrs. Cleever's flourishing milk factory, which does much good and employs much labor, and to the Limerick Clothing Factory, which gives employment to about nine hundred girls and young lads. This establishment, which undertakes government contracts for the supply of uniforms, etc., is one of the largest in the United Kingdom, and is beautifully arranged in all its details for the comfort and convenience of the workers. The Lace School had next to be inspected. The Lace School consists of two rooms in an old building in a squalid part of the city. There are perhaps twenty girls being taught here to make Limerick lace, which threatened to become a lost art until a number of ladies and gentlemen conceived the idea of having the children taught by the surviving lace-makers. The school is in a flourishing condition, and Lady Aberdeen had the pleasure of presenting prizes to the girls that had been won by them for superiority in lace-making. A worker was also selected for the Irish Village, and the lace in process of making for the Exhibition was examined. The first meeting of the new Limerick Committee of the Irish Industries Association had then to be attended, and future work discussed; then various visits to convent and industrial schools in Limerick and some of the commercial establishments in the city, and the day ended with a numerously attended concert on behalf of the hospital.

The following day, as it happened, was Ash Wednesday, and there was some uncertainty about our movements. Was it to be a day of idleness, or a day of work? A day at Killarney, or a day at Clonmel? A day of work, said Lady Aberdeen, and so the party set out for Clonmel, and what we saw well repaid our trouble at Marlfield. About two miles from Clonmel there resides Mrs. Bagwell, whose husband is well known in political and literary circles. This good lady has taught the peasant girls who reside on her husband's property a beautiful form of simple embroidery, samples of which may be seen in the Irish Village. The girls carry on the work at their own hearths, or at the cottage-door on the long summer nights, and when it is completed it is sold for them by Mrs. Bagwell, who overlooks every detail of the industry, paying her workers weekly herself in her own room, and who makes it a condition that a certain portion of the money obtained is lodged in the savings-bank. And thus it is that all these girls have a nice little nest-egg against the day of their marriage; or, if they do not marry, the money is there to fall back upon in old age. Having visited and photographed many of the neat, trim cottages where this embroidery is made and habits of thrift taught, Lady Aberdeen returned to Clonmel, and the same afternoon travelled to Cork, where she became the guest of Sir John and Lady Arnott. A wonderfully gratifying reception awaited her in the southern city. Citizens of every shade of opinion had combined together to form a reception committee, and, in spite of torrents of rain, an assembly of several thousands awaited the train and received their guest with so much enthusiasm that it was with difficulty that the committee could convey her from the railway station to Lady Arnott's carriage, which was in waiting. At an early hour next morning, and in delightful weather, Lady Aberdeen and her party, now accompanied by Lady Arnott and several of the members of her family, journeyed down to Skibbereen by rail. On her arrival there, Lady Aberdeen was presented with an address of welcome by the town commissioners, who, with hundreds of the townspeople, had assembled at the station. The little town had quite a festive appearance, and even the convent was in holiday attire. At this establishment Lady Aberdeen and the other visitors were received by the Bishop of Ross and the Reverend Mother, who, with pardonable pride, pointed to the pleasing spectacle of a large number of young girls industriously engaged at weaving-looms, of which there are twenty-three at present. The girls, who are taught by a Presbyterian weaver from the north of Ireland, manufacture most excellent linens; and there is reason to believe that a fine, healthy weaving-industry will yet be established in the town. When a few nuns and girls can do what we saw in the convent, surely the townspeople, aided by a body like the Irish Industries Association, can do a great deal more.

From this convent Lady Aberdeen drove to Baltimore, a distance of nine miles; but the scenery was charming, and the Countess could not resist the temptation to carry away in her kodak a picture of the beautiful Loughine, an armlet of the sea that wandered inland, and becoming so enamored of the beauty of the hills, resolved to remain there. Loughine is connected with the Atlantic by an outlet or inlet only a few feet broad, so that it appears to be an inland lake. Baltimore is a small village where a number of philanthropic ladies and gentlemen have established a school for instructing boys in the arts connected with the fishing industry. In

A TALK ABOUT IRISH INDUSTRIES IN AN
IRISH VILLAGE.

this good work they have had the assistance of Father Davis, a noble-minded, philanthropic clergyman, the memory of whose services for his fellow-creatures, in that wild and remote region, is his best, and probably his most enduring, monument. Sir Thomas Brady, late government inspector of fisheries, who interests himself also in the promotion of Ireland's fisheries, and Mr. Crosbie of Cork, travelled with the party from Cork and conducted them over the school. The boys showed us how they weave their fishing-nets; and when the local harbour board had presented an address to Lady Aberdeen the party drove back to Skibbereen, and from thence proceeded by rail to Cork. The following morning, at an early hour, visits were paid to several places of interest in " Rebel Cork," as it is called by Irish patriots. The most enjoyable experiences in this connection were at the Convent of the Good Shepherd, where we saw some hundred of little girls, that had been rescued from destitution, knitting, sewing, embroidering, and lace-making. And then ten of them performed for us, in costume, the most graceful country dances and jigs that it would be possible to see. The costumes were Irish, and one of them may be seen in the Irish Village. At 12 o'clock Lady Aberdeen was received by a number of gentlemen at the Munster Agricultural Dairy School, where young men are taught farming and farmers' daughters instructed in all concerning the dairy. Here Lady Aberdeen and Mr. White selected three dairymaids for the Irish Village.

At 1 o'clock the same day, the party left by train for Kinsale. The village people accorded Lady Aberdeen a hearty welcome, and at the convent school the town commissioners presented her with an address. The girls of the school are versed in the art of lace-making and embroidery, and several specimens of their work are on view in the Woman's Building. On returning to Cork, Lady Aberdeen paid a visit to the Protestant Industrial School at Marble Hall, and was conducted over the premises by the Bishop of Cork, Doctor Gregg. The school is flourishing, and the lads happy and well-behaved. The boys invariably do well when they leave this establishment and go out into the world, which speaks well for their training. After leaving Marble Hall Lady Aberdeen made a call at the Convent of the Sisters of Mercy, Blackrock, where the nuns teach the children and the women of the locality to make crochet. Perhaps the very finest Irish point-lace is made in Youghal, so Lady Aberdeen was very much interested in her trip to that fishing-village on the south coast. We left by an early train on Saturday morning, and as usual there was a genuine Irish welcome awaiting the Countess at the station. At the convent school two addresses were presented to her—one from the town commissioners and another from the Board of Guardians. The visitors were then shown the exquisite point-lace made in this school, some of which is on exhibition in the Irish

Village. Before leaving the convent Lady Aberdeen was
presented with a valuable point-lace handkerchief made of
the very finest Irish flax. We returned early in the afternoon in order to be in time for the meeting in Cork which
Lady Aberdeen was to address. For it the most elaborate
preparations had been made, and it was thoroughly successful from every point of view. The large hall in which it was
held was packed with people of every way of political feeling and every religious denomination, and the application
for tickets was largely in excess of the supply. Business
people, professional people, and people who are in the happy

MARLFIELD, COUNTY TIPPERARY.

position of living on their means were all there, and took an
earnest interest in the proceedings. The meeting was
addressed by the most prominent citizens, and an influential
local committee of the Irish Industries Association was
formed to look after the industries of the country and district, and to keep those industries in touch with the parent
association. Lady Aberdeen, in acknowledging the address
presented by the mayor and corporation of Cork, delivered a
powerful speech, in which she graphically described what
the Irish Village would be when completed. She described,
too, the work that was being done by the association of
which she is the president, and to such good purpose that
Sir John Arnott, the proprietor of the *Irish Times*, while she

was yet speaking, intimated his intention to subscribe £100 to the capital for working the Irish Village at the Chicago Exhibition, and £1,000 toward the guarantee fund—an announcement which, of course, was received with ringing cheers.

On Monday before leaving Cork, the excellent school of the Christian Brothers, the convent at Queenstown, where weaving and industrial work are taught, and other institutions were visited, and Blarney was not forgotten, and both Lady Aberdeen and Mr. White kissed the famous stone for the first time by moonlight. Lady Aberdeen addressed a crowded meeting of the friends and members of the Irish Industries Association in Dublin, and on Tuesday, accompanied by Lord Aberdeen, whose engagements now permitted of his return to Ireland, she traveled to New Ross, in County Wexford. The reception accorded to Lord and Lady Aberdeen was enthusiastic in the extreme, for the people turned out in thousands and escorted them through the streets in triumphal fashion, with bands and banners. At the convent school of the Carmelites the town commissioners presented Lady Aberdeen with an address, to which both she and Lord Aberdeen replied, and Mr. White added some earnest words of encouragement to the people to start afresh some centre of work. Wednesday was occupied in paying visits to several places in Dublin where work was being prepared for Chicago, including a convent at Golden Bridge and another at Lakelands, Sandymount; the Model Farm, Glasnevin, and the Hop Stout Factory; and in the evening Lord and Lady Aberdeen departed for London.

From first to last the tour was a success, and undoubtedly it will have a beneficial effect upon Irish industries. That Lady Aberdeen was able to do so much was owing to the admirable arrangements made by Mr. Peter White, the Honorary Secretary of the Irish Industries Association, whose untimely death a few short weeks later came as a painful shock on the myriads of friends whom he had made on both sides of the Atlantic. Lady Aberdeen has herself paid a tribute to his worth and his invaluable services, and her words will fittingly conclude this brief sketch. Speaking on Wednesday, April 19th, at the convent at Cabra to a number of ladies and gentlemen, Lady Aberdeen said, referring to

her previous visit to Dublin: "The remembrances of that
day last in Dublin are altogether sad ones to me, because I
can not help thinking that the exertions which our dear
friend, Mr. Peter White, went through on that day, and the
way in which he exposed himself to the wet, aggravated
very much the illness that had already gained ground on
him, and which in the end deprived us and Ireland of so

TWO OF MRS. BAGWELL'S COTTAGE WORKERS AT MARLFIELD,
COUNTY TIPPERARY.

invaluable a worker. All through that day he had worked
very hard, and in spite of what must have been great phys-
ical discomfort and weakness, although he managed in a great
measure to hide it from us. That day was only a specimen
of what his life had been. Early in the morning he had
been at work at the office; after that he was busy making
arrangements for interviews for me and visits which we had to

pay together. Then he came to Golden Bridge, where we saw the work that had been done there for Chicago, and when we found we could not get here in time, he drove off to tell you I could not come. And he came back quite enthusiastic about all he had seen and the work that was being done here. Then he came with me to Glasnevin Model Farm, and in the afternoon accompanied me to Lakelands Convent at Sandymount. In the evening he saw us off from Kingstown. But that did not complete his day's work, for he went back to the office and continued working, and this was the last day this good friend, who had done so much for Ireland, was ever outside his house. That day was only a specimen of how his life had been spent in working for others. I had

BALTIMORE, COUNTY CORK, NEAR THE INDUSTRIAL FISHERY SCHOOL.

ample opportunity of seeing something of it during that interesting tour which I had through Ireland lately with him for the purpose of seeing the industrial work in various places, and which we were going to represent in Chicago. Wherever we went it was always the same thing; it was Mr. White who did everything, arranged everything, organized everything, and yet he had done it all so tactfully and so unobtrusively that no one scarcely knew it was done at all, and, least of all, that he had done it. And the knowledge he showed everywhere of the different districts, of the needs of those districts, and of the special circumstances connected with them; and the capacity which he showed in bringing his business experience to bear upon the different needs of

PETER WHITE,
HONORABLE SECRETARY OF THE IRISH INDUSTRIES ASSOCIATION, AND MANA-
GER AND ORGANIZER OF THE IRISH VILLAGE AT THE WORLD'S FAIR.
BORN SEPTEMBER, 1850.   DIED APRIL 9, 1893.

the different districts' industries, and the way in which he gave just the right advice, and the way he knew how to give that advice so as to make it always acceptable—all these things make us feel what a terrible and irreparable loss we have sustained, both from the point of view of personal character and mental ability. Never can I hope, for my part, to find a more loyal friend or more efficient and enthusiastic fellow-worker. In saying this I know I am not only speaking for myself, but am voicing the feelings of all my colleagues of the Irish Industries Association.

"A great and abiding sense of blank and loss seems to follow me when I think of him, and more especially to-day, as I came to Ireland for the first time to find him gone, and to remember that I must now set sail for Chicago without him, without his support, his advice, his never-failing wisdom and energy. But while our own great loss thus comes home to us, I know that all our hearts go out to-day in the deepest sympathy to those near and dear ones of his own who are mourning him, his widowed mother, his six little children, and, above all, his brave young wife, who throughout these weary weeks, with their many ups and downs, has shown herself his worthy partner for heroism and unselfishness. Always bright and full of courage, always mindful of the work so dear to his heart, even at the worst times, always desirous to spare others when her whole being was racked with anxiety and apprehensions of the very worst, and even now ready to go out to Chicago to give us the great benefit of her personal help and presence in carrying out the enterprise which her husband had planned and which will, as an Irish newspaper has well put it, form his most fitting monument. It has been good to have been brought into contact with two such heroic lives. I dare not say more, for it seems to me I hear a voice saying, 'Take off thy shoes from off thy feet, for the place whereon thou standest is holy ground.'

"It will be strange indeed if the laying down of his life in our cause does not act as a fresh inspiration to those who are left to carry on the work in his spirit, and if it does not raise up ten workers where there was but one before. This is how he would have had it, and if this proves to be the case, he will not have died in vain; the mystery of his removal at such a time will be mitigated."

BLARNEY CASTLE.

Here is the stone
That whoever kisses,
Oh, he never misses
To grow eloquent.
A clever speaker he'll turn out,
Or an out-and-outer in Parliament.

HOW THE BLARNEY STONE GOT ITS POWER.

The mystic virtues of the world-famed stone in Blarney Castle owe their origin to a truly romantic story.

A nymph of the sunny streams of the South of Ireland became intensely enamoured of the first young prince of the McCarthy family, who at that time ruled over the broad acres of Munster.

Her love was warmly reciprocated, and in this happy state the days and hours rolled smoothly along.

However, in the terrible vicissitudes of his country and kin, the young prince was called away to repel the invaders. The parting was a most affecting one, and mutual promises and vows were exchanged.

During the absence of the young prince the nymph wandered along the banks of the streams of her usual haunts, and, desolate and lonely, awaited with an anxious and longing heart any news from the wars, and in the waning of twilight beguiled the heavy time by singing some of the sweet and melancholy airs of her native music.

In this great anxiety the sad news was brought to her one morning that her lover was slain in battle.

Her grief knew no bounds.

In utter desolation and despair she roamed hither and thither—neither seeking nor accepting comfort nor consolation.

To end this unmeasurable woe she was changed by the superior deity into a stone on the bank of the river on which the castle was afterward built.

The extraordinary virtues which the stone undoubtedly possesses remained undiscovered for many years. But as soon as they were found out the great Cormac McCarthy had the stone placed in what he considered the safest position of his stronghold, and had it guarded with the most jealous care.

THE TRADITIONS OF BLARNEY.

BY J. O'MAHONY.

Wherever the scattered children of the Gael are destined to wander they bring with them, "Through distance and danger, to gladden their hearts like a home-guiding star, the loving memories and abiding traditions of the far-off land—the 'Shan Ban Bocht.' "* Irish men and Irish women, and the many little ones that God sends to bless them, keep ever and always dreaming and hungering after that most distressful country which has been their mother. Thus it is through necessity, as it were, that many of the other people in the wide world have been made acquainted with the stories of the small, green island set in the Western Ocean, whose history has been that of the "Beggar Maid on the Highway of the Universe."

Before Patrick and his white-robed disciples had kindled the light of faith in the land of Erin, Blarney was already a place of importance. In that haunt of sylvan splendor the rock, close within the shadow of the castle, to this day can be traced for the skeptical eye of the modern tourist—the evidence, sure and certain, that there the Druids held their religious festivals and performed their mystic rites. Beside the banks, whereon the cowslips and daffodils grow, of the crystal-clear "Comhan" or Bending Stream there still can be seen the huge Cromlech, which scholars tell us was the Druids' altar. The Castle of Blarney was built by Cormack MacCarthy Laider, that is, "the strong," who died in 1495 and was buried in Kilcrea Abbey in "Muskerry," or the fair country. He was a brave man and a great builder. The MacCarthys are indifferently styled by the historians kings of Desmond and of Cork. One thing is certain: they were a warlike people and very great scorners of death, as were all

---

* The "Shan Ban Bocht," i. e., the poor old woman—a term of endearment for Ireland.

the descendants of that grand old race of men, taller than Roman spears, who in former times held Ireland. When Dermot MacMurrogh brought over Earl Strongbow and his train of adventurous knights, one of these self-same Mac-Carthys, the chief of his nation and captain of his people, Dermot of Cille-Baine, was King of Cork. He was a loose sword, grown old in wars and full of years, for many a fight he won and lost with the Norsemen and Danes who in their strong ships bore down upon his shores. But for all that he "went in" and paid tribute to Henry, the strangers' king. But there was a woman in the case, for the old king, seasoned by seventy winters, was enslaved as a suitor for the fair young hand of a Norman damsel. For her sweet sake he submitted to the English, he suffered the rebellion of his subjects, and subsequently the usurpation of his son. And this was not enough, but even his young bride's friends treated him unfairly, and her *maritagium*, or dower, was withheld for years; which we learn from a curious entry in a close roll preserved in the Tower of London, made in the first year of the reign of Henry III., A. D. 1217—an order to the justiciary of Ireland to cause payment to be made without delay to Petronella de Bloet, a Norman lady, of her dower, which had been given her by her brother, Thomas de Bloet, on her marriage to Dermot MacCarthy, King of Cork. For centuries after the coming of the Normans, the Fitzgeralds, the bravest and proudest of them all, were engaged in continuous warfare with the MacCarthys. It was the spirit of the age; as the old Irish saying has it, "the time of Laebh Laider Arraughter," that is, "of the strong hand uppermost." The annals of Innisfailen tell of many a dark deed of blood that came between these two powerful people.

Once in the winter-time of the year 1267, when night had fallen on the fortified settlement of the strangers at Cullen, in the County of Kerry, the Clancarty, mustering all its horsemen, swooping down in the dark, slew John Fitzgerald and his son Manria, with several knights and many a goodly gentleman of their household, "and so oppressed them," says the pious, cunning-handed annalist, "that the Fitzgerald durst not put a plow to the ground for twelve years after."

4

From such people sprang Cormac the Strong, the brave man
and great builder. His descendants, like his fathers, were
given to warring and "going out upon their keeping," as the
state papers say of them. These, weary of the piping times
of peace, sighed for warfare as the becalmed sailor does for
wind. One of these men, Cormac, son of Dermot, in Queen
Elizabeth's reign, was a source of no little annoyance to the
queen and her council at Dublin. The astute Carew, the
Lord-Governor of Munster, not being able to break this man
by force, endeavored to hurt him by the smoother, if less
straight, ways of diplomacy; but wily and resourceful was
the chieftain with the statesman. Carew kept constantly
writing to her majesty that he had MacCarthy in his power,
as he was agreeing to break through the practice of "Tan-
istry," and come in and have a re-grant of his land from the
crown; but Cormac MacDermot, instead of facilitating the
state policy, kept procrastinating and making soft promises
and raising up delusive delays until in the end Carew became
the laughing-stock of Elizabeth's court, and "Blarney talk"
became proverbial.

With the fall of the Stuarts many an Irish family went
down, and the MacCarthys of Blarney among them. The
estates were confiscated and the heirs sent into exile. Those
were evil days for the remnant of the old stock which still
clung closely to the religion of their fathers. The sons of
many of the noble houses went out upon the outlaw's wild
career as "Rapparees" in the woods and upon the hillsides, but
most of them went beyond the seas as captains of the "Wild
Geese"—the Irish recruits which swelled the continental
armies and won victories from "Dunkirque to Belgrade."
Even in Ireland to-day many of the stories of these brave
men and their adventures obtain. Some of the sweetest
songs in the kindly pleasure-giving Gaelic are the Jacobite
relics. Mr. Denny Lane of Cork, who was the friend of
Thomas Davis and stood on the outer circle of the wonderful
body of men who helped to bring a new soul into their
country, after the famine of 1847, composed a beautiful
ballad, typical of its kind, purporting to be the lament of an
Irish maiden for her lover who has gone to France with the
"Wild Geese:"

The heath is brown on Carrighdhown,
  The clouds are dark on Ardualee,
And many a stream comes rushing down
  To swell the angry Ouingabwee.
The mountain blast is sweeping fast
  Through many a leafless tree,
But I'm alone, for he has gone,
  My hawk is flown, Ochone Machree!

The heath was green on Carrighdhown,
  Bright shone the sun on Ardualee,
The dark green trees bent trembling down
  To kiss the strawberry, Ouingabwee;
That happy day, 'twas but last May,
  It's like a dream to me,
When Donal swore, aye, o'er and o'er,
  We'd part no more, Asthore Machree!

Soft April showers and sweet May flowers
  May bring the summer back again,
But will they bring me back the hours
  I spent with my brave Donal then?
It's but a chance, for he's gone to France
  To wear the fleur de lys,
But I'll follow you, my Donal, dhu.
  For still I'm true to you, Machree!

When Cromwell was in Ireland Broghill (1643) took Blarney, as Donogh, son of Cormac, was identified with the confederation of Kilkenny, and in 1796 the last Earl of Clancarthy was outlawed and his estate escheated for his interest in Righ Shamus. The immortal Father Prout, the author of the charter song of Cork, "The Bells of Shandon," in his relique giving an account of Walter Scott's visit to Blarney and kissing the stone, in 1823, gives us polyglot versions of the Groves of Blarney, which was written by Dick Milliken, a yeomanry captain in the famous North Cork Militia, who made themselves so notorious against the boys of Wexford in the troubled times of '98. Dick Milliken's pastoral air, "The Groves of Blarney," that never sufficiently to be encored song, according to Mahony, describes—

              The groves of Blarney
              That look so charming,
              Down by the purlings
              Of sweet silent brooks,
              Are decked by posies,

> That spontaneous grow there,
> Planted in order
> In the rocky nooks.
> It's there the daisy
> And the sweet carnations,
> The blooming pink,
> And the rose so fair,
> Likewise the lily
> And the daffodilly,
> All flowers that scent
> The sweet open air.

The old-time poet then proceeds to tell us:

> There is a cave where
> No daylight enters,
> But bats and badgers
> Are forever bred,
> And moss by nature
> Makes it completer
> Than a coach and six
> Or a downy bed.

And admits that there are—

> Lots of beauties
> Which I can not entwine,
> But were I a preacher
> In every feature
> I'd make 'em shine.
> There is a stone
> That whoever kisses,
> Oh! he never misses
> To grow eloquent.
> 'Tis he may clamber
> To a lady's favor,
> Or become a member
> Of Parliament;
> A clever spouter
> He'll sure turn out, or
> An out-and-outer
> To be let alone.
> Don't try to hinder him,
> Or to bewilder him,
> For he's a pilgrim
> From the Blarney stone.

When the estate was confiscated it fell into the hands of
the Jeffers family, who came into Ireland with the William-

ites.   Father Prout preserves for us also the humorous song
sung to the racy air, " I'm Akin to the Callaghans:"

"BLARNEY CASTLE, ME DARLIN'."

Och Blarney Castle, me darlint,
  Sure ye're nothing at all but a stone
Wrapt in ivy—a nest for all vermint,
  Since the old Lord Clancarty is gone.

Bad cess to that robber. ould Cromwell
  Himself and his long battering train,
That rambled o'er here like a porpoise
  In two or three hookers from Spain.

With his Jack-boots he stepped on the water,
  And he walked clane right over the lake,
While his sodgers they all followed after,
  As dry as a duck and a drake.

Then the gates he burned down to a cinder,
  And the roof he demolished likewise:
Oh the rafters they flamed out like tinder,
  And the building flamed up to the skies.

And he gave the estate to the Jeffers,
  With the dairy, the cows, and the hay:
And they lived there in clover like heifers,
  As their ancestors do to this day.

So much for the songs and skits on Blarney.

The close keep or central tower, which is the main portion of the old castle standing, has the famous stone.   This
stone, according to tradition, is endowed with the property
of communicating to the happy tongue that comes in contact with its polished surface the gift of gentle, insinuating
speech, with soft talk and all its ramifications—such as lead
captive the female heart, or elaborate mystifications of a
graver grain—such as may do for the House of Commons—
are characterized by the mysterious term, "Blarney."

The beautiful lake on the southern side of the building
was dragged many years ago by an eccentric member of the
Jeffers family, who thought to drain it and discover the
plate which tradition says the McCarthys hid there in their
flight after the siege of Blarney by Cromwell, in trust that
times of greater hope would arise and they would have their

own again. Tradition says that only three McCarthys knew the exact whereabouts of this treasure, and when one is dying he communicates it to another faithful one of the *gens*. The peasant people of Blarney tell weird stories, especially about its lake, in which the supernatural preponderate. The husbandman hastening home at night sees the shore of the lake crowded with rich cattle, which vanish into the air on closer examination, and the hill at Bawnafenn (or the " Pasture of Beauty ") about the lake, the country girl who sings while she milks the quiet kine hears her voice rivaled by the beautiful singing of a woman's voice beneath the lake, and when she hushes her song to listen more attentively, it too dies away upon the breeze.

We do not know whether the new Blarney by the shores of Lake Michigan will bring whispering voices and shades from the unseen world, but we do know that the Irishmen and Irishwomen who linger around its precincts will hear murmurs from the " ould country " which will tell them that by their presence here they are bringing help and blessings to the homes of their kinsmen in the Emerald Isle.

THE COTTAGE INDUSTRIES OF DONEGAL.

BY MISS KATHERINE TYNAN.

AFTER one quits the region of railways at Ballyshannon, Donegal becomes a county of hills and dales. Ballyshannon one leaves in the valley, by the exquisite banks of its silver Erne, with all its gracious memories of William Allingham; and one is raced by "the brave pony," as its driver calls it, of the mail-car, up a break-neck hill, and into the swelling county beyond. For long it is wild and bare enough, but one brown shoulder of a hill is looming ever over another, and on the horizon one catches sight of the sea like a flashing silver shield; and the brown fields are full of lakelets of limpid water that mirror the sky—these April days of an extraordinary brilliancy—so the scene is never without its beauty. Curiously depopulated, however! It is only at intervals of a couple of miles, that one comes on a haggard, handsome peasant sowing his corn, or a poor hamlet by the roadside. Here there are the cottage industries of Mrs. Hamilton of Ballintra; but one wonders, looking over the lovely landscape, where are the cottagers to be taught, or whether the Celt be not indeed vanished from the face of this lovely, unfruitful land. It adds to the sparseness and solitariness that the fences are stone walls, the stones heaped with a looseness and carelessness that make one suppose the first west wind from the Atlantic would bring them clattering about the sods. An exceedingly lovely desert, with its April banks of violets and primroses, and its brilliant April sky. Toward Donegal town the country takes a different aspect. It becomes more green and cultivated, and the closer hills of the Donegal highlands loom great and sapphire-like. There are park-lands and deep plantations covering the hillside. Every wild rush down a hillside or up into the world brings one to a new beauty. Now one turns a corner to find the river Esk widening to the sea; the encroaching tide has sapped the cultivated land, and sends up a long tongue of salt marshes into the valley. The principal portion of Donegal town is built about a triangle—the Diamond, they call it. One approaches this from the quay, where the tall spars of ships are graceful against the silver distance; and the abbey where the Four Masters wrote their annals looks from its graves out over the water. In Donegal one comes on the first track of the cottage industries. Mr. Magee, who has a big shop at the corner of the Diamond, is an extensive buyer of the woolen fabrics that are brought from the outlying districts to be sold in Ardara market. He has a great stock of brown and gray tweeds, Donegal homespuns, which he sells extensively in English and American markets. He told us that at the market held on the first of each month at Ardara, the average purchases amount to £1,000 worth. He himself signed cheques for £300 at the last market, and he is only one of the buyers. The stuffs are of great purity and durability, and the patterns, so far as they go, are good. But they do not go far enough. The people go on making their everlasting browns and grays, in stripes and squares; and meanwhile every year Fashion, as eager for new things as the Athenians of old, demands a change; and so the Donegal homespuns, in their groove of sameness, go to the wall. New patterns are needed urgently, says Mr. Magee; new dyes, improved machines, and a couple of skilled weavers to teach new ways.

Another industry one hears of at Donegal is embroidering on muslin and linen. Mr. Hugh Gallagher of the Quay had piles of fine cambric handkerchiefs, sprigged and lettered by the peasants of Donegal. He is only the middleman for these, which go to merchants in Belfast, or to more distant markets. There was a great demand in America for such goods till the McKinley tariff—which Donegal fondly hopes will be repealed under a Cleveland administration—ruined this delicate industry so far as America is concerned.

Donegal now sends away her comely sons and daughters. Everywhere one hears the same sad story of emigration; everywhere resounds the cry, " If the people could only be kept in the country!" What they want is manufactures and such industries as sewing, embroidering, and lace-making. Very curiously, Ireland is condemned to be a solely agricultural country, seeing that in most of her area, and especially in the west, the climate is against the crops. Such a brilliant day as we had driving from Ballyshannon to Donegal is rare. Far oftener it is as we saw it to day—its hills gray, its peat-fields black, its lakes leaden under a leaden sky. It is lovely under rain, with all the sad, deep color, and in the distance the hills blurred silverly, with an illusion about them as if they had swathed their great purple forms in unutterably lovely webs of gossamer. Often we saw the women stooping patiently over the black potato-ridges, sowing the potatoes. The men are at work on Mr. Balfour's light railway, which winds in and out all that road from Donegal to Killybegs. It will be opened in June, and will bring Donegal near the markets. It is because of their present absorption in field labor that Mr. Gallagher had only embroidered cambric handkerchiefs to show us. It is the sparsest time of year for his embroideries. At other times he would have pillow-shams, bedspreads, doilies, table-centres, and all the other delightful things in embroidered linen. The number of girls and women he has employed averages 1,500. At a busy time it may be 2,000. He pays them about 1s. 4d. a dozen for embroidering an initial letter. They can earn about 10d. a day at it—a miserable pittance, one thinks; but where there are three or four daughters in a family, a little gold mine to people as unfamiliar with money as the Donegal peasants. While I was talking with Mr. Gallagher, one of his embroideresses came in; a tidily dressed girl, with a gentle Donegal face. They are so gentle, by the by, a woman might take a journey, as unprotected as Tom Moore's damsel of "Rich and Rare," through Donegal, and meet with as exquisite courtesy as in that age of gold. They are all charming, from the old women, full of bows and smiles, who instruct you on your way with an affectionate hand on your arm, and a "You're welcome, indeed!" to the children, who, with no eye to backsheesh, trot half a street to show you the place you want, turning all the while on you grave eyes that disarm in you the least suspicion of mockery. They are not at all shy, those children; only very serious. They impart facts in the domestic history of "him" or "her"

Lyka-ne-Grena (the Sunny Nook), Lady Aberdeen's Cottage at the Irish Village,
Reproduced from a Cottage at Rushbrook, near Queenstown,
from which this Photograph was taken.

you are about to visit, in a shrill Northern accent, which somewhat baffles the dull comprehension of one unused to it.
Donegal people all tighten their lips as they speak, to let
out the pronunciation in that thin Scotch fashion.

Across the "Diamond" is a shirt agency, where a clever
young lady from a Derry firm instructs neophytes in the
shirt-making and receives and gives out work. This industry does not go very far, for the shirts are only finished
by the Donegal workers, but it dispenses some £10 a
week, and is quite a business-like little traffic. It helps to
keep those dove-eyed girls at home amid their hills and in
the pure air, with its delicious reek of turf-smoke. In their
Donegal valleys they are safe, though the diet may be low
and the damp neuralgic. The thought of God is there, and
the church-bell floats the Angelus over all the stony fields;
and there is the simple, human love which is so strong with
them. Out in the world Sin goes by with roses in her hair,
and beckoning, beckoning, while here is the guardian angel
and the innocent lives. Let them stay, in God's name. Their
hills are safest and happiest.

Meanwhile the country, so cruelly ungrateful to the tiller,
is bursting with mineral wealth, and many other resources.
Stony capital, somewhere in a foreign city, has locked all
this away from the people. A coal mine is sold unworked
to an English company that will not have its monopoly
interfered with; a copper mine is elsewhere under these
rocky surfaces. The rosy salmon are for a London market.
The harbours are empty and half-choked by the shifting
sands.

At Killybegs we found Mr. Neil McLoone, one of the
principal buyers of the homespuns. His very insufficient
store is piled high with them in various degrees of color and
finish. One beautiful stuff is a soft, fleecy gray, with a blue
line in it. The whole piece of this was going to an English
marquis. Mr. McLoone's son goes out in the wide world for
orders, not only to Dublin and London, but to Paris and the
Continent. We have a card of his couched in elegant
French: "*Manufacturier de Tweeds, filés et tissés à domi-
cile, faits de couleurs naturelles et de couleurs teintes à domi-
cile.*" Presently, when the light railroad is working, I sup-

pose Mr. McLoone's facilities will be much improved. He, with the brothers Magee and Mr. Neil McNelis of Ardara, are the principal buyers. These homespun woollens is the industry of Donegal that is, at present, most on a business basis, and deserves to be, for anything more genuine in the way of manufacture could not well be imagined. Your Donegal weaver has not yet advanced to the knowledge of shoddy.

Between Killybegs and Kilcar, and in all the mountains along the seaboard, the sprigging industry is carried on—a poor industry, dying hard from starvation. It was on the drive we began to realize the misery of the Donegal peasants. They ask the earth for bread, and for answer she gives them a stone. No one can realize those stones unless he has first seen them. Frequently a mountain-side is so serried with their battalions, that man has retired hopelessly from the contest. Yet in seemingly the most awful deserts there are sparse spaces of black plowed land—plowed and harrowed by those patient men and women—while the boulders that forced themselves to the surface have been piled by an infinite amount of labor into stone ditches, as the loose wall of stones is called. Yet amid the black earth the gaunt, gray monsters lift themselves, and claim what is their own, what has been desert, and will be desert, despite that puny creature, man, his labour and his sweat. In Donegal nearly all those peasants walk with bent backs like very old men, while the old men! oh, they have long forgotten to be straight, and toil away, with figures as unnaturally bent as some of those distorted bushes by the seashore, blown all one way and into gnarled age by the steady whip of the sea-winds. Those stony fields impress the visitor more than anything. Now and then the hopelessly sterile have been walled off, and are the receptacles of some of the overflow of their neighbors. Such fields! Coming from Dublin County and its rich land, one wondered indeed at the squalid spaces—about the size of your table-cloth, dear madam. By the roadside were enormous rocks that one would have deemed it past the strength of man to lift from the earth. Everywhere was the same arid depopulation—the only sign of life a crooked figure in the fields, or a cabin in which it is a crying shame for God's image to be housed.

Kilcar is at the foot of one of those steep mountain-roads. It is the center of the sprigging industry for those parts. Mrs. Gallagher and her daughter Mary give out the handkerchiefs and other things for the embroidering, and pay for the work. Their little shop would make a delightful *genre* picture. The dainty purity that was in the cap and apron of the old woman was mirrored in everything in the shop, down to the show placards of grocers and purveyors, for this was a general shop, as well as a sprigging agency. The goods, patterned, arrive in great heaps from the Belfast wholesale house, to which the goods are consigned. So there is no picking up of bargains in the Donegal Mountains. The Belfast firm does not pay as well as Mr. Gallagher of Donegal, who has a special market for the sprigged goods. They are paid for so miserably, indeed, that a good sprigger can only earn a shilling a week! The old story of the McKinley tariff shutting the goods from the American markets, for not long ago sprigging was a tremendous industry here. Where the agency nowadays pays a beggarly ten-pound note among these myriad mountains and glens, it was formerly a thousand. If prayers can obtain the repeal of the McKinley tariff, I feel sure the Donegal peasants will bring it about.

At Kilcar one can see that majestic monster Slieve Liag extending its mighty human face into the clouds. It is nearly always a phantom of the mists, for the clouds stoop low and trail upon it, swathing its awfulness as it lies recumbent upon the plain like a great dead god, whose fighting is over and whose apotheosis is to lie forever in so splendid a state. Down near its base are the curing-stations of Teelin, established by the Congested Districts Board. This board makes roads and advances money for boat-buying and housebuilding; it even seeks to improve the cocks and hens of the district by the importation of a new strain—less hardy, say the people, who do not yet understand the importance of improving the standard of the poultry, if they are to be looked to as a permanent source of profit. Those curing-stations for the fish are a great boon, and things need not be so bad in those places and at those times that the men are engaged in the fishing. But Donegal fishing, like the summer tourist, is a variable quantity. Fishing, except in the really settled weather, is out of the question. Visit the superb Muckros caves, two miles from Kilcar, and in a brilliant day of soft sunshine you will be able to imagine what the winter storms are like. If you are startled now at the mighty creatures, arching themselves in all their green, shining length for a spring, what will it be in winter when the sea rises, literally, mountains high—and climbing pillar and wall and roof of the caves, that are like new rock temples of the East—swarms up the land, high into the farmers' fields that are yet strewn with sea-shells. Sea-weed, too, was high in the fields, and we came upon them drying it for manure. At the farmer's house there we saw the spinning-wheel, an implement that would excite unbounded admiration in a Belgravian drawing-room, especially with a lovely head above it, a lovely hand placing the threads, and a foot "like the new moon," as Coventry Patmore says, deftly moving to and fro. It would not be easy, however, to surpass the farmer's daughter, with her graceful, smooth, brown head, her gray eyes with their sky-bright glances, and the softly blushing cheeks. All the women here who do not sprig, spin in their off moments. The day we were at Muckros, however, they were cutting seed-potatoes in the farm-house kitchen, and the old mother kept a chronically discontented look because surprised out of the usual tidiness of the house place. Carrick lies under the shadow of Slieve Liag, which, as we drove in the dusk, was wreathed in soaring mists. There is a very fine and tolerably expensive hotel at Carrick. No doubt if one sought health or pleasure in this exquisite vale, it would not be difficult to find a lodging in the village or in an adjacent farm-house. At Carrick there is a fairly flourishing woolen industry, like all Donegal industries somewhat in need of extension and fostering. The Donegal peasants are quick and expert knitters. There is an agency in Carrick which distributes and receives work for a wholesale merchant, Mr. Patterson of London. The knitted goods are chiefly for ladies and children — combinations, petticoats, combined bodices and skirts, children's gloves, gaiters, woolen boots, etc. We saw several rooms piled high with the goods, and beautiful goods they are.

Very often there are two colors used; blue and pink, pink and white, pink and gray, make charming mixtures. The women knit so rapidly that they take only two days to a petticoat, and correspondingly little time to the other things. This agency pays from £10 to £12 pounds a week among the poor people about Carrick. But after all, even supposing them full of work—an impossible thing, perhaps, where there is so little work to be given and so many able and willing hands stretched out for it—the best of them all could not earn more than 4 shillings a week or so. The parish priest of Carrick has the usual tale of the people's abject poverty, though the next priest will tell you how much better off Carrick is, because of its fishing station, than his poor parish.

The next parish to Carrick—or the next priest to the P. P. of Carrick, rather—was the curate of Glencolumbkille. The Glen Head is one of the sights of Donegal, so I suppose many tourists come in contact with the heart-rending poverty of Glencolumbkille. All about the valley, under the magnificent bold Head, lie the scattered little cottages, clinging to the mountain-side like a starling's nest under the eaves. From this priest, a cultivated and refined gentleman who stood out in lonely prominence amid his poor flock, we heard the old miserable famine cry. They have eaten their seed-potatoes in Glencolumbkille, and there are none to put into the unyielding earth. Last season was one of many wet and cold, and the potatoes rotted in the earth. Those that were saved had to be eaten. They were sprigging in the cottages at their shilling a week. Up in the glen a weaver, a haggard-faced, handsome man, was plying his old-fashioned cumbrous loom in a Rembrandt-like interior, dark with the turf smoke. At the window his wife sat and spun, her brown head and crimson-shawled shoulders outlined against the little square. They have just one alleviation of hardship in Donegal—fuel is always in plenty. But half the cottages have no chimney—just a hole in the thatch to let the smoke through, and all the four winds that blow puff the smoke back into the cabins. This weaver's yarn was black with the turf smoke. How he was to bring his webs to the Ardara market on the first of the month, clean and saleable, baffled one's comprehension. They showed us in this cottage the moss from which they make one of their dyes, the *crottle*, to give it the phonetic spelling. I have said moss, but it is rather a lichen which grows on the rocks by the sea. Another dye which gives streaks of brown and orange is made by boiling the heather; yet a third from steeping the stuffs in bog water impregnated with iron, as is so much water in Donegal. The peat, so impregnated, used to be an industry. It was used in gas-works for some purpose or other. Of late years Germany, importing something cheaper, has beaten it out of the market, but there are signs of its revival, they say. The dye made from the red ironized bog water is called *dubachta*. Kelp-gathering, too, is something of an industry on this coast, but a poor and precarious one.

I suppose the Glen Head must rise nearly 2,000 feet. It will remain with one as a memory, the majestic scenery and the poor human hives below. These cotters, like the rest of the people of the Donegal Highlands, are descendants of the native Irish, driven hither from the fertile plains at the time of the Ulster plantations. They and their children paid dearly, God knows, for faith and country.

We left our poor young priest there, with his intellect and aspirations, lonely in a scene of beauty to make one melancholy mad, and with the people's hunger knocking at his heart. The drive from Glencolumbkille, past the pillar stones where the saint made his stations, and up and down the great chain of mountains that intersect Donegal at this point, is full of wild beauty. Now you are climbing a mountain-side by a road, one side of which is walled with rock, the other sheer precipice; again you are flying down the other side, having topped the summit by a causeway of road suspended high above the stony bog. Clattering down one such road, we saw a sight that made us hold our breath. The great hills, near and distant, were in gold and silver haze, and though to us the sun was invisible, he was streaming from some rift straight upon them in belts of rosy fire, stretching for miles across flank and summit. As we drove on, the rosy wonder resolved itself into mere sunshine that seemed in comparison poor and prosaic.

Not far from Ardara, after crossing a great stretch of barren moorland, one crests the brow of a hill and descends into the incomparably magnificent Glengeish. I am quite sure that the world can have no glen more lovely. The path goes down as down the side of a house, winding slowly beneath cliffs that rise each side from 1,200 to 1,800 feet. A singing stream brawls over stones far down, and is fed by a hundred rivulets that wind in and out in little cascades and shallow pools down the mountain-side. I can not imagine people going to Switzerland while there is Glengeish in Donegal.

Ardara is the great market for the cloth. Like all the Donegal villages, it climbs down one hill and up another. In Ardara the great authority on the weaving is Mr. Neil McNelis of the hotel, the principal buyer in this district. You will see the stuffs here, rough or silky, all in soft, harmonious colors and delightful to the touch. The weavers in Donegal are sorely hampered by the old looms they are so conservative about abandoning. Many and many a web of cloth they spoil, and one can not but believe that the young men would be glad to abandon the unchancy things for something better if they but had the opportunity.

In Ardara we saw also some of the stockings for which the district is famous. Glenties is the centre for the stocking-knitting, and there there is an immense trade in them done by the brothers McDevitt. We missed inspecting Messrs. McDevitt's stores and stock by the accident of our passing through Glenties on a Sunday; but the gloves and stockings we saw at Mr. Kennedy's of Ardara were of the same kind, all beautifully knitted and of the most recent colors and patterns.

At Ardara we heard, too, of an industry fast dying out. This is the weaving of a mixture of linen and woolen for ladies' dresses, the result of which was described to us so enthusiastically that we could scarcely help feeling a great desire to see the gowns so eloquently described. It seems at present to be made only at Downstrand, or Narin, on the seashore, and is not offered for sale, though the country gentry often make use of it. Ardara, by Glenties to Dungloe, is a repetition of the scenery of cliffs and stony crags, except-

5

ing that when one has climbed the steep hill from Dooras
Bridge and got on the long moorland road that runs five or
six miles to Dungloe, one is in the midst of a chain of beautiful lakes. They are on each side of the bog road, now little
and solitary, again widening to embrace many little islands.
In Dungloe again they have the stockings, supplemented by
jerseys for fishermen and others, and of course the inevitable
gloves. In Dungloe, Sweeneys of the Hotel are large
employers, and are quite ready to show their stock to any
one interested. Miss Sweeney told us the people are very
quick in devising patterns for the knittings, taking the
squares and diamonds of wall-papers, tiles, or anything else
that may come their way. Some of the stockings are well
paid for, the best at 3s. 4d. a pair; and as an expert knitter can
knit a stocking in a day, the work, if there were sufficient
demand, would be very paying.

Between Dungloe and Gweedore one comes on the stony
territory of the Rosses, where Miss Roberts carries on her
knitting industries, which employ so many workers, and which
are largely sold by the Irish Industries Association. It is
hard to imagine without seeing it the great aridity of this
desert. It seems little enough peopled, unlike Gweedore,
which is a perfect hive of cabins. It, too, is mainly
composed of great slabs of stone, covering their acres,
with pathetic bits of tillage running up against the great boulders. It is at Gweedore one sees the little fields. A good-
sized pocket-handkerchief would cover some of them. The
glen, however, from end to end, and it must be many miles
in extent, overflows with people, and the houses are cleanly
white-washed. They pasture through the glen little lean
cattle, and hardy, clever mountain-sheep that are as much at
home among the dogs and the children as is the pig in other
parts of Ireland. They are a very tall and handsome race
up at Gweedore, with straight, regular features and much
dignity of look. The women of the North are delightfully
clean—quite shining in their frilled caps—and they nearly
all wear the scarlet petticoats which make them look so
picturesque out in the fields. All the women were out in
the fields as we went through the country. I believe there is
horrible poverty really in Gweedore, but there is great

purity of living. Whisky is little known. The priest, who is king of Gweedore, and I really believe the one responsible for sheltering all those chickens under the wing of their mountains, has warred on the whisky so determinedly that it has all but disappeared. Gweedore people live by their little cattle, their sheep, the potatoes, and the fishing. It is near here, at Bunbeg, that Mrs. Ernest Hart has her factory and technical school, and the headquarters of the various operations of the well-known Donegal Industrial Fund. In the cottages there are few industries—the only one with any vitality is the eternal knitting. They won't change their knitting for anything else, those conservative folk. They may be artistic as to their own particular pursuit, but turn them to any other and they are, perhaps willfully, dull. There are a few old weavers in the glen, about a dozen in all; but they only work for the country people. This is all there is of cottage industries. The one who knows them and their needs best says: "Give them a market in their midst first of all—such a market as Ardara, for example. Then give them some communication with the outer world. A light railway would be a gift from heaven. If they had the market all Gweedore would be a-whirr with the spinning-wheel, the loom, and the click of the needles. And such a one as Coll of Bunbeg need not be sitting idle, with his four looms hidden away and his five braw weaver-sons doing farm labor in Scotland." He says his case is the same as that of all the old weavers in the glen. It is all pitiable. Here they are so ready for work—work, not charity, good folk!

After Donegal one ceases to wonder at the supremacy of the priests among the Irish peasants. In such places as Columbkille and Gweedore, what would they be without their priests? Leaves blown before the storm—sheep shepherdless in such a snow as buries these mountains.

On the priest's bookshelves you will often see law and medicine by the side of his theology. He is the real friend to them, and all the world outside the careless and unreal.